# Let 'Em Breathe Space!

Lester Del Rey

**Alpha Editions**

This edition published in 2022

ISBN : 9789356718913

Design and Setting By
**Alpha Editions**
www.alphaedis.com
Email - info@alphaedis.com

# LET'EM BREATHE SPACE!

Eighteen men and two women in the closed world of a space ship for five months can only spell tension and trouble—but in this case, the atmosphere was *literally* poisoned.

Five months out from Earth, we were half-way to Saturn and three-quarters of the way to murder. At least, I was. I was sick of the feuding, the worries and the pettiness of the other nineteen aboard. My stomach heaved at the bad food, the eternal smell of people, and the constant sound of nagging and complaints. For ten lead pennies, I'd have gotten out into space and tried walking back to Earth. Sometimes I thought about doing it without the pennies.

But I knew I wasn't that tough, in spite of what I looked. I'd been built to play fullback, and my questionable brunet beauty had been roughed up by the explosion years before as thoroughly as dock fighting on all the planets could have done. But sometimes I figured all that meant was that there was more of me to hurt, and that I'd had more experience screaming when the anodyne ran out.

Anyhow, whole-wheat pancakes made with sourdough for the ninth "morning" running was too damned much! I felt my stomach heave over again, took one whiff of the imitation maple syrup, and shoved the mess back fast while I got up faster.

---

It was a mistake. Phil Riggs, our scrawny, half-pint meteorologist, grinned nastily and reached for the plate. "'Smatter, Paul? Don't you like your breakfast? It's good for you—whole wheat contains bran. The staff of life. Man, after that diet of bleached paste...."

---

There's one guy like that in every bunch. The cook was mad at us for griping about his coffee, so our group of scientists on this cockeyed Saturn Expedition were getting whole wheat flour as punishment, while Captain Muller probably sat in his cabin chuckling about it. In our agreement, there was a clause that we could go over Muller's head on such things with a unanimous petition—but Riggs had spiked that. The idiot liked bran in his flour, even for pancakes!

Or else he was putting on a good act for the fun of watching the rest of us suffer.

"You can take your damned whole wheat and stuff it—" I started. Then I shrugged and dropped it. There were enough feuds going on aboard the cranky old *Wahoo*! "Seen Jenny this morning, Phil?"

He studied me insolently. "She told Doc Napier she had some stuff growing in hydroponics she wanted to look at. You're wasting your time on that babe, boy!"

"Thanks for nothing," I muttered at him, and got out before I really decided on murder. Jenny Sanderson was our expedition biologist. A natural golden blonde, just chin-high on me, and cute enough to earn her way through a Ph. D. doing modelling. She had a laugh that would melt a brass statue and which she used too much on Doc Napier, on our chief, and even on grumpy old Captain Muller—but sometimes she used it on me, when she wanted something. And I never did have much use for a girl who was the strong independent type where there was a man to do the dirty work, so that was okay.

I suppose it was natural, with only two women among eighteen men for month after month, but right then I probably liked Doc Napier less than the captain, even. I pulled myself away from the corridor to hydroponics, started for observation, and then went on into the cubbyhole they gave me for a cabin. On the *Wahoo*, all a man could do was sleep or sit around and think about murder.

Well, I had nobody to blame but myself. I'd asked for the job when I first heard Dr. Pietro had collected funds and priorities for a trip to study Saturn's rings at close hand. And because I'd done some technical work for him on the Moon, he figured he might as well take me as any other good all-around mechanic and technician. He hadn't asked me, though—that had been my own stupid idea.

Paul Tremaine, self-cure expert! I'd picked up a nice phobia against space when the super-liner *Lauri Ellu* cracked up with four hundred passengers on my first watch as second engineer. I'd gotten free and into a suit, but after they rescued me, it had taken two years on the Moon before I could get up nerve for the shuttle back to Earth. And after eight years home, I should have let well enough alone. If I'd known anything about Pietro's expedition, I'd have wrapped myself in my phobia and loved it.

But I didn't know then that he'd done well with priorities and only fair with funds. The best he could afford was the rental of the old Earth-Mars-Venus triangle freighter. Naturally, when the *Wahoo's* crew heard they were slated for what would be at least three years off Earth without fancy bonus rates, they quit. Since nobody else would sign on, Pietro had used his priorities to get an injunction that forced them back aboard. He'd stuffed extra oxygen, water, food and fertilizer on top of her regular supplies, then, filled her holds with some top level fuel he'd gotten from a government assist, and set out. And by the time I found out about it, my own contract was iron-bound, and I was stuck.

As an astrophysicist, Pietro was probably tops. As a man to run the Lunar Observatory, he was a fine executive. But as a man to head up an expedition into deep space, somebody should have given him back his teething ring.

Not that the *Wahoo* couldn't make the trip with the new fuel; she'd been one of the early survey ships before they turned her into a freighter. But she was meant for a crew of maybe six, on trips of a couple of months. There were no game rooms, no lounges, no bar or library—nothing but what had to be. The only thing left for most of us aboard was to develop our hatreds of the petty faults of the others. Even with a homogeneous and willing crew, it was a perfect set-up for cabin fever, and we were as heterogeneous as they came.

Naturally the crew hated the science boys after being impressed into duty, and also took it out on the officers. The officers felt the same about both other groups. And the scientists hated the officers and crew for all the inconveniences of the old *Wahoo*. Me? I was in no-man's land—technically in the science group, but without a pure science degree; I had an officer's feelings left over from graduating as an engineer on the ships; and I looked like a crewman.

It cured my phobia, all right. After the first month out, I was too disgusted to go into a fear funk. But I found out it didn't help a bit to like space again and know I'd stay washed up as a spaceman.

We'd been jinxed from the start. Two months out, the whole crew of scientists came down with something Doc Napier finally diagnosed as food poisoning; maybe he was right, since our group ate in our own mess hall, and the crew and officers who didn't eat with us didn't get it. Our astronomer, Bill Sanderson, almost died. I'd been lucky, but then I never did react to things much. There were a lot of other small troubles, but the next major trick had been fumes from the nuclear generators getting up into our quarters—it was always our group that had the trouble. If Eve Nolan hadn't been puttering with some of her trick films at the time—she and Walt Harris had the so-called night shift—and seen them blacken, we'd have been dead before they discovered it. And it took us two weeks of bunking with the sullen crew and decontamination before we could pick up life again. Engineer Wilcox had been decent about helping with it, blaming himself. But it had been a mess.

Naturally, there were dark hints that someone was trying to get us; but I couldn't see any crewman wiping us out just to return to Earth, where our contract, with its completion clause, would mean he wouldn't have a dime coming to him. Anyhow, the way things were going, we'd all go berserk before we reached Saturn.

The lunch gong sounded, but I let it ring. Bullard would be serving us whole wheat biscuits and soup made out of beans he'd let soak until they turned sour. I couldn't take any more of that junk, the way I felt then. I heard some of the men going down the corridor, followed by a confused rumble of voices. Then somebody let out a yell. "Hey, *rooob!*"

That meant something. The old yell spacemen had picked up from carney people to rally their kind around against the foe. And I had a good idea of who was the foe. I heard the yell bounce down the passage again, and the slam of answering feet.

Then the gravity field went off. Or rather, was cut off. We may have missed the boat in getting anti-gravity, if there is such a thing, but our artificial gravity is darned near foolproof.

It was ten years since I'd moved in free fall, but Space Tech had done a good job of training good habits. I got out of my bunk, hit the corridor with a hand out, bounced, kicked, and dove toward the mess hall without a falter. The crewmen weren't doing so well—but they were coming up the corridor fast enough.

I could have wrung Muller's neck. Normally, in case of trouble, cutting gravity is smart. But not here, where the crew already wanted a chance to commit mayhem, and had more experience than the scientists.

Yet, surprisingly, when I hit the mess hall ten feet ahead of the deckhands, most of the scientists were doing all right. Hell, I should have known Pietro, Sanderson and a couple others would be used to no-grav; in astronomical work, you cut your eye teeth on that. They were braced around the cook, who huddled back in a corner, while our purser-steward, Sam, was still singing for help.

The fat face of the cook was dead white. Bill Sanderson, looking like a slim, blond ballet dancer and muscled like an apache expert, had him in one hand and was stuffing the latest batch of whole wheat biscuits down his throat. Bill's sister, Jenny, was giggling excitedly and holding more biscuits.

The deckhands and Grundy, the mate, were almost at the door, and I had just time enough to slam it shut and lock it in their faces. I meant to enjoy seeing the cook taken down without any interruption.

Sam let out a final yell, and Bullard broke free, making a mess of it without weight. He was sputtering out bits of the biscuit. Hal Lomax reached out a big hand, stained with the chemicals that had been his life's work, and pushed the cook back.

And suddenly fat little Bullard switched from quaking fear to a blind rage. The last of the biscuit sailed from his mouth and he spat at Hal. "You damned hi-faluting black devil. You—*you* sneering at my cooking. I'm a white man, I am—I don't have to work for no black ni...."

I reached him first, though even Sam started for him then. You can deliver a good blow in free-fall, if you know how. His teeth against my knuckles stopped my leap, and the back of his head bounced off the wall. He was unconscious as he drifted by us, moving upwards. My knuckles stung, but it had been worth it. Anyhow, Jenny's look more than paid for the trouble.

The door shattered then, and the big hulk of Mate Grundy tumbled in, with the two deckhands and the pair from the engine room behind him. Sam let out a yell that sounded like protest, and they headed for us—just as gravity came on.

I pulled myself off the floor and out from under Bullard to see the stout, oldish figure of Captain Muller standing in the doorway, with Engineer Wilcox slouched easily beside him, looking like the typical natty space officer you see on television. Both held gas guns.

"All right, break it up!" Muller ordered. "You men get back to your work. And you, Dr. Pietro—my contract calls for me to deliver you to Saturn's moon, but it doesn't forbid me to haul you the rest of the way in irons. I won't have this aboard my ship!"

Pietro nodded, his little gray goatee bobbing, his lean body coming upright smoothly. "Quite right, Captain. Nor does it forbid me to let you and your men spend the sixteen months on the moon—where *I* command—in irons. Why don't you ask Sam what happened before you make a complete fool of yourself, Captain Muller?"

Sam gulped and looked at the crew, but apparently Pietro was right; the little guy had been completely disgusted by Bullard. He shrugged apologetically. "Bullard insulted Dr. Lomax, sir. I yelled for someone to help me get him out of here, and I guess everybody got all mixed up when gravity went off, and Bullard cracked his head on the floor. Just a misunderstanding, sir."

Muller stood there, glowering at the cut on my knuckles, and I could feel him aching for a good excuse to make his threat a reality. But finally, he grunted and swung on his heel, ordering the crew with him. Grundy threw us a final grimace and skulked off behind him. Finally there was only Wilcox, who grinned, shrugged, and shut the door quietly behind him. And we were left with the mess free-fall had made of the place.

I spotted Jenny heading across the room, carefully not seeing the fatuous glances Pietro was throwing her way, and I swung in behind. She nodded back at me, but headed straight for Lomax, with an odd look on her face. When she reached him, her voice was low and businesslike.

"Hal, what did those samples of Hendrix's show up?"

Hendrix was the Farmer, in charge of the hydroponics that turned the carbon dioxide we breathed out back to oxygen, and also gave us a bit of fresh vegetables now and then. Technically, he was a crewman, just as I was a scientist; but actually, he felt more like one of us.

Lomax looked surprised. "What samples, Jenny? I haven't seen Hendrix for two weeks."

"You—" She stopped, bit her lip, and frowned. She swung on me. "Paul, have you seen him?"

I shook my head. "Not since last night. He was asking Eve and Walt to wake him up early, then."

"That's funny. He was worried about the plants yesterday and wanted Hal to test the water and chemical fertilizer. I looked for him this morning, but when he didn't show up, I thought he was with you, Hal. And—the plants are dying!"

"All of them?" The half smile wiped off Hal's face, and I could feel my stomach hit my insteps. When anything happens to the plants in a ship, it isn't funny.

She shook her head again. "No—about a quarter of them. I was coming for help when the fight started. They're all bleached out. And it looks like—like chromazone!"

That really hit me. They developed the stuff to fight off fungus on Venus, where one part in a billion did the trick. But it was tricky stuff; one part in ten-million would destroy the chlorophyll in plants in about twenty hours, or the hemoglobin in blood in about fifteen minutes. It was practically a universal poison.

Hal started for the door, then stopped. He glanced around the room, turned back to me, and suddenly let out a healthy bellow of seeming amusement. Jenny's laugh was right in harmony. I caught the drift, and tried to look as if we were up to some monkey business as we slipped out of the room. Nobody seemed suspicious.

Then we made a dash for hydroponics, toward the rear of the ship. We scrambled into the big chamber together, and stopped. Everything looked normal among the rows of plant-filled tanks, pipes and equipment. Jenny led us down one of the rows and around a bend.

The plants in the rear quarter weren't sick—they were dead. They were bleached to a pale yellow, like boiled grass, and limp. Nothing would save them now.

"I'm a biologist, not a botanist—" Jenny began.

Hal grunted sickly. "Yeah. And I'm not a life hormone expert. But there's one test we can try."

He picked up a pair of rubber gloves from a rack, and pulled off some wilted stalks. From one of the healthy tanks, he took green leaves. He mashed the two kinds together on the edge of a bench and watched. "If it's chromazone, they've developed an enzyme by now that should eat the color out of those others."

In about ten seconds, I noticed the change. The green began to bleach before my eyes.

Jenny made a sick sound in her throat and stared at the rows of healthy plants. "I checked the valves, and this sick section is isolated. But—if chromazone got into the chemicals.... Better get your spectroanalyzer out, Hal, while I get Captain Muller. Paul, be a dear and find Hendrix, will you?"

I shook my head, and went further down the rows. "No need, Jenny," I called back. I pointed to the shoe I'd seen sticking out from the edge of one of the tanks. There was a leg attached.

I reached for it, but Lomax shoved me back. "Don't—the enzymes in the corpse are worse than the poison, Paul. Hands off." He reached down with the gloves and heaved. It was Hendrix, all right—a corpse with a face and hands as white as human flesh could ever get. Even the lips were bleached out.

Jenny moaned. "The fool! The stupid fool. He *knew* it was dangerous without gloves; he suspected chromazone, even though none's supposed to be on board. And I warned him . . ."

"Not against this, you didn't," I told her. I dropped to my knees and took another pair of gloves. Hendrix's head rolled under my grasp. The skull was smashed over the left eye, as if someone had taken a sideswipe at Hendrix with a hammer. No fall had produced that. "You should have warned him about his friends. Must have been killed, then dumped in there."

"Murder!" Hal bit the word out in disgust. "You're right, Paul. Not too stupid a way to dispose of the body, either—in another couple of hours, he'd have started dissolving in that stuff, and we'd never have guessed it was murder. That means this poisoning of the plants wasn't an accident. Somebody poisoned the water, then got worried when there wasn't a report on the plants; must have been someone who thought it worked faster on plants than it does. So he came to investigate, and Hendrix caught him fooling around. So he got killed."

"But who?" Jenny asked.

I shrugged sickly. "Somebody crazy enough—or desperate enough to turn back that he'll risk our air and commit murder. You'd better go after the captain while Hal gets his test equipment. I'll keep watch here."

It didn't feel good in hydroponics after they left. I looked at those dead plants, trying to figure whether there were enough left to keep us going. I studied Hendrix's body, trying to tell myself the murderer had no reason to come back and try to get me.

I reached for a cigarette, and then put the pack back. The air felt almost as close as the back of my neck felt tense and unprotected. And telling myself it was all imagination didn't help—not with what was in that chamber to keep me company.

# II

Muller's face was like an iceberg when he came down—but only after he saw Hendrix. Before then I'd caught the fat moon-calf expression on his face, and I'd heard Jenny giggling. Damn it, they'd taken enough time. Hal was already back, fussing over things with the hunk of tin and lenses he treated like a newborn baby.

Doc Napier came in behind them, but separately. I saw him glance at them and look sick. Then both Muller and Napier began concentrating on business. Napier bent his nervous, bony figure over the corpse, and stood up almost at once. "Murder all right."

"So I guessed, Dr. Napier," Muller growled heavily at him. "Wrap him up and put him between hulls to freeze. We'll bury him when we land. Tremaine, give a hand with it, will you?"

"I'm not a laborer, Captain Muller!" Napier protested. I started to tell him where he could get off, too.

But Jenny shook her head at us. "Please. Can't you see Captain Muller is trying to keep too many from knowing about this? I should think you'd be glad to help. Please?"

Put that way, I guess it made sense. We found some rubber sheeting in one of the lockers, and began wrapping Hendrix in it; it wasn't pleasant, since he was beginning to soften up from the enzymes he'd absorbed. "How about going ahead to make sure no one sees us?" I suggested to Jenny.

Muller opened his mouth, but Jenny gave one of her quick little laughs and opened the door for us. Doc looked relieved. I guessed he was trying to kid himself. Personally, I wasn't a fool—I was just hooked; I knew perfectly well she was busy playing us off against one another, and probably having a good time balancing the books. But hell, that's the way life runs.

"Get Pietro up here!" Muller fired after us. She laughed again, and nodded. She went with us until we got to the 'tween-hulls lock, then went off after the chief. She was back with him just as we finished stuffing Hendrix through and sealing up again.

Muller grunted at us when we got back, then turned to Lomax again. The big chemist didn't look happy. He spread his hands toward us, and hunched his shoulders. "A fifty-times over-dose of chromazone in those tanks— fortunately none in the others. And I can't find a trace of it in the fertilizer chemicals or anywhere else. Somebody deliberately put it into those tanks."

"Why?" Pietro asked. We'd filled him in with the rough details, but it still made no sense to him.

"Suppose you tell me, Dr. Pietro," Muller suggested. "Chromazone is a poison most people never heard of. One of the new *scientific* nuisances."

Pietro straightened, and his goatee bristled. "If you're hinting . . ."

"I am *not* hinting, Dr. Pietro. I'm telling you that I'm confining your group to their quarters until we can clean up this mess, distil the water that's contaminated, and replant. After that, if an investigation shows nothing, I *may* take your personal bond for the conduct of your people. Right now I'm protecting my ship."

"But captain—" Jenny began.

Muller managed a smile at her. "Oh, not you, of course, Jenny. I'll need you here. With Hendrix gone, you're the closest thing we have to a Farmer now."

---

"Captain Muller," Pietro said sharply. "Captain, in the words of the historical novelists—drop dead! Dr. Sanderson, I forbid you to leave your quarters so long as anyone else is confined to his. I have ample authority for that."

"Under emergency powers—" Muller spluttered over it, and Pietro jumped in again before he could finish.

"Precisely, Captain. Under emergency situations, when passengers aboard a commercial vessel find indications of total irresponsibility or incipient insanity on the part of a ship's officer, they are considered correct in assuming command for the time needed to protect their lives. We were poisoned by food prepared in your kitchen, and were nearly killed by radioactivity through a leak in the engine-room—and no investigation was made. We are now confronted with another situation aimed against our welfare—as the others were wholly aimed at us—and you choose to conduct an investigation against our group only. My only conclusion is that you wish to confine us to quarters so we cannot find your motives for this last outrage. Paul, will you kindly relieve the captain of his position?"

They were both half right, and mostly wrong. Until it was proved that our group was guilty, Muller couldn't issue an order that was obviously discriminatory and against our personal safety in case there was an attack directed on us. He'd be mustered out of space and into the Lunar Cells for that. But on the other hand, the "safety for passengers" clause Pietro was citing applied only in the case of overt, direct and physical danger by an officer to normal passengers. He might be able to weasel it through a court, or he might be found guilty of mutiny. It left me in a pretty position.

Jenny fluttered around. "Now, now—" she began.

I cut her off. "Shut up, Jenny. And you two damned fools cool down. Damn it, we've got an emergency here all right—we may not have air plants enough to live on. Pietro, we can't run the ship—and neither can Muller get through what's obviously a mess that may call for all our help by confining us. Why don't you two go off and fight it out in person?"

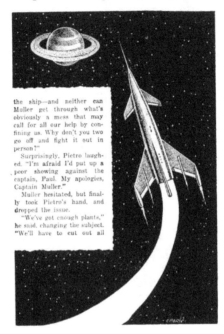

Surprisingly, Pietro laughed. "I'm afraid I'd put up a poor showing against the captain, Paul. My apologies, Captain Muller."

Muller hesitated, but finally took Pietro's hand, and dropped the issue.

"We've got enough plants," he said, changing the subject. "We'll have to cut out all smoking and other waste of air. And I'll need Jenny to work the hydroponics, with any help she requires. We've got to get more seeds planted, and fast. Better keep word of this to ourselves. We—"

A shriek came from Jenny then. She'd been busy at one of the lockers in the chamber. Now she began ripping others open and pawing through things inside rubber-gloves. "Captain Muller! The seeds! The seeds!"

Hal took one look, and his face turned gray.

"Chromazone," he reported. "Every bag of seed has been filled with a solution of chromazone! They're worthless!"

"How long before the plants here will seed?" Muller asked sharply.

"Three months," Jenny answered. "Captain Muller, what are we going to do?"

The dour face settled into grim determination. "The only sensible thing. Take care of these plants, conserve the air, and squeeze by until we can reseed. And, Dr. Pietro, with your permission, we'll turn about for Earth at once. We can't go on like this. To proceed would be to endanger the life of every man aboard."

"Please, Danton." Jenny put her hand on Pietro's arm. "I know what this all means to you, but—"

Pietro shook her off. "It means the captain's trying to get out of the expedition, again. It's five months back to Earth—more, by the time we kill velocity. It's the same to Saturn. And either way, in five months we've got this fixed up, or we're helpless. Permission to return refused, Captain Muller."

"Then if you'll be so good as to return to your own quarters," Muller said, holding himself back with an effort that turned his face red, "we'll start clearing this up. And not a word of this."

Napier, Lomax, Pietro and I went back to the scientists' quarters, leaving Muller and Jenny conferring busily. That was at fifteen o'clock. At sixteen o'clock, Pietro issued orders against smoking.

Dinner was at eighteen o'clock. We sat down in silence. I reached for my plate without looking. And suddenly little Phil Riggs was on his feet, raving. "Whole wheat! Nothing but whole wheat bread! I'm sick of it—sick! I won't—"

"Sit down!" I told him. I'd bitten into one of the rolls on the table. It was white bread, and it was the best the cook had managed so far. There was corn instead of baked beans, and he'd done a fair job of making meat loaf. "Stop making a fool of yourself, Phil."

He slumped back, staring at the white bun into which he'd bitten. "Sorry. Sorry. It's this air—so stuffy. I can't breathe. I can't see right—"

Pietro and I exchanged glances, but I guess we weren't surprised. Among intelligent people on a ship of that size, secrets wouldn't keep. They'd all put bits together and got part of the answer. Pietro shrugged, and half stood up to make an announcement.

---

"Beg pardon, sirs." We jerked our heads around to see Bullard standing in the doorway.

He was scared stiff, and his words got stuck in his throat. Then he found his voice again. "I heard as how Hendrix went crazy and poisoned the plants and went and killed himself and we'll all die if we don't find some trick, and what I want to know, please, sirs, is are what they're saying right and you know all kinds of tricks and can you save us because I can't go on like this not knowing and hearing them talking outside the galley and none of them telling me—"

Lomax cut into his flood of words. "You'll live, Bullard. Farmer Hendrix did get killed in an accident to some of the plants, but we've still got air enough. Captain Muller has asked the help of a few of us, but it's only a temporary emergency."

Bullard stared at him, and slowly some of the fear left his face—though not all of it. He turned and left with a curt bow of his head, while Pietro added a few details that weren't exactly lies to Lomax's hasty cover-up, along with a grateful glance at the chemist. It seemed to work, for the time being—at least enough for Riggs to begin making nasty remarks about cooked paste.

Then the tension began to build again. I don't think any of the crew talked to any of our group. And yet, there seemed to be a chain of rumor that exchanged bits of information. Only the crew could have seen the dead plants being carried down to our refuse breakdown plant; and the fact it was chromazone poisoning must have been deduced from a description by some of our group. At any rate, both groups knew all about it—and a little bit more, as was usual with rumors—by the second day.

Muller should have made the news official, but he only issued an announcement that the danger was over. When Peters, our radioman-navigator, found Sam and Phil Riggs smoking and dressed them down, it didn't make Muller's words seem too convincing. I guessed that Muller had other things on his mind; at least he wasn't in his cabin much, and I didn't see Jenny for two whole days.

My nerves were as jumpy as those of the rest. It isn't too bad cutting out smoking; a man can stand imagining the air is getting stale; but when every unconscious gesture toward cigarettes that aren't there reminds him of the air, and when every imagined stale stench makes him want a cigarette to relax, it gets a little rough.

Maybe that's why I was in a completely rotten mood when I finally did spot Jenny going down the passage, with the tight coveralls she was wearing emphasizing every motion of her hips. I grabbed her and swung her around. "Hi, stranger. Got time for a word?"

She sort of brushed my hand off her arm, but didn't seem to mind it. "Why, I guess so, Paul. A little time. Captain Muller's watching the 'ponics."

"Good," I said, trying to forget Muller. "Let's make it a little more private than this, though. Come on in."

She lifted an eyebrow at the open door of my cabin, made with a little giggle, and stepped inside. I followed her, and kicked the door shut. She reached for it, but I had my back against it.

"Paul!" She tried to get around me, but I wasn't having any. I pushed her back onto the only seat in the room, which was the bunk. She got up like a spring uncoiling. "Paul Tremaine, you open that door. You know better than that. Paul, please!"

"What makes me any different than the others? You spend plenty of time in Muller's cabin—and you've been in Pietro's often enough. Probably Doc Napier's, too!"

Her eyes hardened, but she decided to try the patient and reason-with-the-child line. "That is different. Captain Muller and I have a great deal of business to work out."

"Sure. And he looks great in lipstick!"

It was a shot in the dark, but it went home. I wished I'd kept my darned mouth shut; before I'd been suspecting it—now I knew. She turned pink and tried to slap me, which won't work when the girl is sitting on a bunk and I'm on my feet. "You mind your own business!"

"I'm doing that. Generations should stick together, and he's old enough to be your father!"

She leaned back and studied me. Then she smiled slowly, and something about it made me sick inside. "I like older men, Paul. They make people my own age seem so callow, so unfinished. It's so comforting to have mature people around. I always did have an Electra complex."

"The Greeks had plenty of names for it, kid," I told her. "Don't get me wrong. If you want to be a slut, that's your own business. But when you pull the innocent act on me, and then fall back to sophomore psychology—"

This time she stood up before she slapped. Before her hand stung my face, I was beginning to regret what I'd said. Afterwards, I didn't give a damn. I picked her up off the floor, slapped her soundly on the rump, pulled her tight against me, and kissed her. She tried scratching my face, then went passive, and wound up with one arm around my neck and the other in the hair at the back of my head. When I finally put her down she sank back onto the bunk, breathing heavily.

"Why, Paul!" And she reached out her arms as I came down to meet them. For a second, the world looked pretty good.

Then a man's hoarse scream cut through it all, with the sound of heavy steps in panic flight. I jerked up. Jenny hung on. "Paul.... Paul...." But there was the smell of death in the air, suddenly. I broke free and was out into the corridor. The noise seemed to come from the shaft that led to the engine room, and I jumped for it, while I heard doors slam.

This time, there was a commotion, like a wet sack being tossed around in a pentagonal steel barrel, and another hoarse scream that cut off in the middle to a gargling sound.

---

I reached the shaft and started down the center rail, not bothering with the hand-grips. I could hear something rustle below, followed by silence, but I couldn't see a thing; the lights had been cut.

I could feel things poking into my back before I landed; I always get the creeps when there's death around, and that last sound had been just that—somebody's last sound. I *knew* somebody was going to kill me before I could find the switch. Then I stumbled over something, and my hair stood on end. I guess my own yell was pretty horrible. It scared me worse than I was already. But my fingers found the switch somehow, and the light flashed on.

Sam lay on the floor, with blood still running from a wide gash across his throat. A big kitchen knife was still stuck in one end of the horrible wound. And one of his fingers was half sliced off where the blade of a switch-blade shiv had failed on him and snapped back.

Something sounded above me, and I jerked back. But it was Captain Muller, coming down the rail. The man had obviously taken it all in on the way down. He jerked the switch-blade out of Sam's dead grasp and looked at the point of the knife. There was blood further back from the cut finger, but none on the point.

"Damn!" Muller tossed it down in disgust. "If he'd scratched the other man, we'd have had a chance to find who it was. Tremaine, have you got an alibi?"

"I was with Jenny," I told him, and watched his eyes begin to hate me. But he nodded. We picked Sam up together and lugged his body up to the top of the shaft, where the crowd had collected. Pietro, Peters, the cook, Grundy and Lomax were there. Beyond them, the dark-haired, almost masculine head of Eve Nolan showed, her eyes studying the body of Sam as if it were a negative in her darkroom; as usual, Bill Sanderson was as close to her as he could get. But there was no sign now of Jenny. I glanced up the corridor but saw only Wilcox and Phil Riggs, with Walt Harris trailing them, rubbing the sleep out of his eyes.

Muller moved directly to Pietro. "Six left in my crew now, Dr. Pietro. First Hendrix, now Sam. Can you still say that the attack is on *your* crew—when mine keep being killed? This time, sir, I demand . . ."

"Give 'em hell, Captain," ape-man Grundy broke in. "Cut the fancy stuff, and let's get the damned murdering rats!"

Muller's eyes quartered him, spitted his carcass, and began turning him slowly over a bed of coals. "Mister Grundy, I am master of the *Wahoo*. I fail to remember asking for your piratical advice. Dr. Pietro, I trust you will have no objections if I ask Mr. Peters to investigate your section and group thoroughly?"

"None at all, Captain Muller," Pietro answered. "I trust Peters. And I feel sure you'll permit me to delegate Mr. Tremaine to inspect the remainder of the ship?"

Muller nodded curtly. "Certainly. Until the madman is found, we're all in danger. And unless he is found, I insist I must protect my crew and my ship by turning back to Earth."

"I cannot permit that, sir!"

"Your permission for that was not requested, Dr. Pietro! Yes, Bullard?"

The cook had been squirming and muttering to himself for minutes. Now he darted out toward Grundy, and his finger pointed to Lomax. "He done it! I seen him. Killed the only friend I had, he did. They went by my galley—and—and he grabbed my big knife, that one there. And he killed Sam."

---

"You're sure it was Lomax?" Muller asked sharply.

"Sure I'm sure. Sam, he was acting queer lately. He was worried. Told me he saw something, and he was going to know for sure. He borrowed my switch-blade knife that my wife gave me. And he went out looking for something. Then I heard him a-running, and I looked up, and there was this guy, chasing him. Sure, I seen him with my own eyes."

Eve Nolan chuckled throatily, throwing her mannish-cut hair back from her face. She was almost pretty with an expression on her countenance, even if it was amused disgust. "Captain Muller, that's a nice story. But Dr. Lomax was with me in my darkroom, working on some spectroanalysis slides. Bill Sanderson and Phil Riggs were waiting outside for us. And Mr. Peters saw us come out together when we all ran down here."

Peters nodded. Muller stared at us for a second, and the hunting lust died out of his eyes, leaving them blank and cold. He turned to Bullard. "Bullard, an explanation might make me reduce your punishment. If you have anything to say, say it now!"

The cook was gibbering and actually drooling with fear. He shook, and sweat popped out all over him. "My knife—I hadda say something. They stole my knife. They wanted it to look like I done it. God, Captain, you'da done the same. Can't punish a man for trying to save his life. I'm a good man, I am. Can't whip a good man! Can't—"

"Give him twenty-five lashes with the wire, Mr. Grundy," Muller said flatly.

Pietro let out a shriek on top of the cook's. He started forward, but I caught him. "Captain Muller's right," I told him. "On a spaceship, the full crew is needed. The brig is useless, so the space-enabling charter recognizes flogging. Something is needed to maintain discipline."

Pietro dropped back reluctantly, but Lomax faced the captain. "The man is a coward, hardly responsible, Captain Muller. I'm the wounded party in this case, but it seems to me that hysteria isn't the same thing as maliciousness. Suppose I ask for clemency?"

"Thank you, Dr. Lomax," Muller said, and actually looked relieved. "Make it ten lashes, Mr. Grundy. Apparently no real harm has been done, and he will not testify in the future."

Grundy began dragging Bullard out, muttering about damn fool groundlubbers always sticking their noses in. The cook caught at Lomax's hand on the way, literally slobbering over it. Lomax rubbed his palm across his thigh, looking embarrassed.

Muller turned back to us. "Very well. Mr. Peters will begin investigating the expedition staff and quarters; Mr. Tremaine will have free run over the rest of the ship. And if the murderer is not turned up in forty-eight hours, we head back to Earth!"

Pietro started to protest again, but another scream ripped down the corridor, jerking us all around. It was Jenny, running toward us. She was breathing hoarsely as she nearly crashed into Dr. Pietro.

Her face was white and sick, and she had to try twice before she could speak.

"The plants!" she gasped out. "Poison! They're dying!"

# III

It was chromazone again. Muller had kept most of the gang from coming back to hydroponics, but he, Jenny, Pietro, Wilcox and myself were enough to fill the room with the smell of sick fear. Now less than half of the original space was filled with healthy plants. Some of the tanks held plants already dead, and others were dying as we watched; once beyond a certain stage, the stuff acted almost instantly—for hours there was only a slight indication of something wrong, and then suddenly there were the dead, bleached plants.

Wilcox was the first to speak. He still looked like some nattily dressed hero of a space serial, but his first words were ones that could never have gone out on a public broadcast. Then he shrugged. "They must have been poisoned while we were all huddled over Sam's body. Who wasn't with us?"

"Nonsense," Pietro denied. "This was done at least eighteen hours ago, maybe more. We'd have to find who was around then."

"Twenty hours, or as little as twelve," Jenny amended. "It depends on the amount of the dosage, to some extent. And...." She almost managed to blush. "Well, there have been a lot of people around. I can't even remember. Mr. Grundy and one of the men, Mr. Wilcox, Dr. Napier—oh, I don't know!"

Muller shook his head in heavy agreement. "Naturally. We had a lot of work to do here. After word got around about Hendrix, we didn't try to conceal much. It might have happened when someone else was watching, too. The important thing, gentlemen, is that now we don't have reserve enough to carry us to Saturn. The plants remaining can't handle the air for all of us. And while we ship some reserve oxygen...."

He let it die in a distasteful shrug. "At least this settles one thing. We have no choice now but to return to Earth!"

"Captain Muller," Pietro bristled quickly, "that's getting to be a monomania with you. I agree we are in grave danger. I don't relish the prospect of dying any more than you do—perhaps less, in view of certain peculiarities! But it's now further back to Earth than it is to Saturn. And before we can reach either, we'll have new plants—or we'll be dead!"

"Some of us will be dead, Dr. Pietro," Wilcox amended it. "There are enough plants left to keep some of us breathing indefinitely."

Pietro nodded. "And I suppose, in our captain's mind, that means the personnel of the ship can survive. Captain Muller, I must regard your constant attempt to return to Earth as highly suspicious in view of this recurrent sabotage of the expedition. Someone here is apparently either a complete madman or so determined to get back that he'll resort to anything to accomplish his end. And you have been harping on returning over and over again!"

Muller bristled, and big heavy fist tightened. Then he drew himself up to his full dumpy height. "Dr. Pietro," he said stiffly, "I am as responsible to my duties as any man here—and my duties involve protecting the life of every man and woman on board; if you wish to return, I shall be *most* happy to submit this to a formal board of inquiry. I—"

"Just a minute," I told them. "You two are forgetting that we've got a problem here. Damn it, I'm sick of this fighting among ourselves. We're a bunch of men in a jam, not two camps at war now. I can't see any reason why Captain Muller would want to return that badly."

Muller nodded slightly. "Thank you, Mr. Tremaine. However, for the record, and to save you trouble investigating there is a good reason. My company is now building a super-liner; if I were to return within the next six months, they'd promote me to captain of that ship—a considerable promotion, too."

For a moment, his honesty seemed to soften Pietro. The scientist mumbled some sort of apology, and turned to the plants. But it bothered me; if Muller had pulled something, the smartest thing he could have done would be to have said just what he did.

Besides, knowing that Pietro's injunction had robbed him of a chance like that was enough to rankle in any man's guts and make him work up something pretty close to insanity. I marked it down in my mental files for the investigation I was supposed to make, but let it go for the moment.

Muller stood for a minute longer, thinking darkly about the whole situation. Then he moved toward the entrance to hydroponics and pulled out the ship speaker mike. "All hands and passengers will assemble in hydroponics within five minutes," he announced. He swung toward Pietro. "With your permission, Doctor," he said caustically.

The company assembled later looked as sick as the plants. This time, Muller was hiding nothing. He outlined the situation fully; maybe he shaded it a bit to throw suspicion on our group, but in no way we could pin down. Finally he stated flatly that the situation meant almost certain death for at least some of those aboard.

"From now on, there'll be a watch kept. This is closed to everyone except myself, Dr. Pietro, Mr. Peters, and Dr. Jenny Sanderson. At least one of us will be here at all times, equipped with gas guns. Anyone else is to be killed on setting foot inside this door!" He swung his eyes over the group. "Any objections?"

---

Grundy stirred uncomfortably. "I don't go for them science guys up here. Takes a crazy man to do a thing like this, and everybody knows...."

Eve Nolan laughed roughly. "Everybody knows you've been swearing you won't go the whole way, Grundy. These jungle tactics should be right up your alley."

"That's enough," Muller cut through the beginnings of the hassle. "I trust those I appointed—at least more than I do the rest of you. The question now is whether to return to Earth at once or to go on to Saturn. We can't radio for help for months yet. We're not equipped with sharp beams, we're low powered, and we're off the lanes where Earth's pick-ups hunt. Dr. Pietro wants to go on, since we can't get back within our period of safety; I favor returning, since there is no proof that this danger will end with this outrage. We've agreed to let the result of a vote determine it."

Wilcox stuck up a casual hand, and Muller nodded to him. He grinned amiably at all of us. "There's a third possibility, Captain. We can reach Jupiter in about three months, if we turn now. It's offside, but closer than anything else. From there, on a fast liner, we can be back on Earth in another ten days."

Muller calculated, while Peters came up to discuss it. Then he nodded. "Saturn or Jupiter, then. I'm not voting, of course. Bullard is disqualified to vote by previous acts." He drew a low moan from the sick figure of Bullard for that, but no protest. Then he nodded. "All those in favor of Jupiter, your right hands please!"

I counted them, wondering why my own hand was still down. It made some sort of sense to turn aside now. But none of our group was voting— and all the others had their hands up, except for Dr. Napier. "Seven," Muller announced. "Those in favor of Saturn."

Again, Napier didn't vote. I hesitated, then put my hand up. It was crazy, and Pietro was a fool to insist. But I knew that he'd never get another chance if this failed, and....

"Eight," Muller counted. He sighed, then straightened. "Very well, we go on. Dr. Pietro, you will have my full support from now on. In return, I'll expect every bit of help in meeting this emergency. Mr. Tremaine was correct; we cannot remain camps at war."

Pietro's goatee bobbed quickly, and his hand went out. But while most of the scientists were nodding with him, I caught the dark scowl of Grundy, and heard the mutters from the deckhands and the engine men. If Muller could get them to cooperate, he was a genius.

Pietro faced us, and his face was serious again. "We can hasten the seeding of the plants a little, I think, by temperature and light-and-dark cycle manipulations. Unfortunately, these aren't sea-algae plants, or we'd be in comparatively little trouble. That was my fault in not converting. We can, however, step up their efficiency a bit. And I'm sure we can find some way to remove the carbon dioxide from the air."

"How about oxygen to breathe?" Peters asked.

"That's the problem," Pietro admitted. "I was wondering about electrolyzing water."

Wilcox bobbed up quickly. "Can you do it on AC current?"

Lomax shook his head. "It takes DC."

"Then that's out. We run on 220 AC. And while I can rectify a few watts, it wouldn't be enough to help. No welders except monatomic hydrogen torches, even."

Pietro looked sicker than before. He'd obviously been counting on that. But he turned to Bullard. "How about seeds? We had a crop of tomatoes a month ago—and from the few I had, they're all seed. Are any left?"

Bullard rocked from side to side, moaning. "Dead. We're all gonna be dead. I told him, I did, you take me out there, I'll never get back. I'm a good man, I am. I wasn't never meant to die way out here. I—I—"

He gulped and suddenly screamed. He went through the door at an awkward shuffle, heading for his galley. Muller shook his head, and turned toward me. "Check up, will you, Mr. Tremaine? And I suggest that you and Mr. Peters start your investigation at once. I understand that chromazone would require so little hiding space that there's no use searching for it. But if you can find any evidence, report it at once."

Peters and I left. I found the galley empty. Apparently Bullard had gone to lie on his stomach in his bunk and nurse his terror. I found the freezer compartments, though—and the tomatoes. There must have been a bushel of them, but Bullard had followed his own peculiar tastes. From the food he served, he couldn't stand fresh vegetables; and he'd cooked the tomatoes down thoroughly and run them through the dehydrator before packing them away!

---

It was a cheerful supper, that one! Bullard had half-recovered and his fear was driving him to try to be nice to us. The selection was good, beyond the inevitable baked beans; but he wasn't exactly a chef at best, and his best was far behind him. Muller had brought Wilcox, Napier and Peters down to our mess with himself, to consolidate forces, and it seemed that he was serious about cooperating. But it was a little late for that.

Overhead, the fans had been stepped up to counteract the effect of staleness our minds supplied. But the whine of the motors kept reminding us our days were counted. Only Jenny was normal; she sat between Muller and Pietro, where she could watch my face and that of Napier. And even her giggles had a forced sound.

There were all kinds of things we could do—in theory. But we didn't have that kind of equipment. The plain fact was that the plants were going to lose the battle against our lungs. The carbon dioxide would increase, speeding up our breathing, and making us all seem to suffocate. The oxygen would grow thinner and thinner, once our supplies of bottled gas ran out. And eventually, the air wouldn't support life.

"It's sticky and hot," Jenny complained, suddenly.

"I stepped up the humidity and temperature controls," I told her. She nodded in quick comprehension, but I went on for Muller's benefit. "Trying to give the plants the best growing atmosphere. We'll feel just as hot and sticky when the carbon dioxide goes up, anyhow."

"It must already be up," Wilcox said. "My two canaries are breathing faster."

"Canaries," Muller said. He frowned, though he must have known of them. It was traditional to keep them in the engine-room, though the reason behind it had long since been lost. "Better kill them, Mr. Wilcox."

Wilcox jerked, and his face paled a bit. Then he nodded. "Yes, sir!"

That was when I got scared. The idea that two birds breathing could hurt our chances put things on a little too vivid a basis. Only Lomax seemed unaffected. He shoved back now, and stood up.

"Some tests I have to make, Captain. I have an idea that might turn up the killer among us!"

I had an idea he was bluffing, but I kept my mouth shut. A bluff was as good as anything else, it seemed.

At least, it was better than anything I seemed able to do. I prowled over the ship, sometimes meeting Peters doing the same, but I couldn't find a bit of evidence. The crewmen sat watching with hating eyes. And probably the rest aboard hated and feared us just as much. It wasn't hard to imagine the man who was behind it all deciding to wipe one of us out. My neck got a permanent crimp from keeping one eye behind me. But there wasn't a shred of evidence I could find.

In two more days, we began to notice the stuffiness more. My breathing went up enough to notice. Somehow, I couldn't get a full breath. And the third night, I woke up in the middle of my sleep with the feeling something was sitting on my chest; but since I'd taken to sleeping with the light on, I saw that it was just the stuffiness that was bothering me. Maybe most of it had been psychological up until then. But that was the real thing.

The nice part of it was that it wouldn't be sudden—we'd have days to get closer and closer to death; and days for each one to realize a little more that every man who wasn't breathing would make it that much easier for the rest of us. I caught myself thinking of it when I saw Bullard or Grundy.

Then trouble struck again. I was late getting to the scene this time, down by the engine room. Muller and Bill Sanderson were ahead of me, trying to separate Hal Lomax and Grundy, and not doing so well. Lomax brought up a haymaker as I arrived, and started to shout something. But Grundy was out of Muller's grasp, and up, swinging a wrench. It connected with a dull thud, and Lomax hit the floor, unconscious.

I picked Grundy up by the collar of his jacket, heaved him around and against a wall, where I could get my hand against his esophagus and start squeezing. His eyeballs popped, and the wrench dropped from his hands. When I get mad enough to act that way, I usually know I'll regret it later. This time it felt good, all the way. But Muller pushed me aside, waiting until Grundy could breathe again.

"All right," Muller said. "I hope you've got a good explanation, before I decide what to do with you."

Grundy's eyes were slitted, as if he'd been taking some of the Venus drugs. But after one long, hungry look at me, he faced the captain. "Yes, sir. This guy came down here ahead of me. Didn't think nothing of it, sir. But when he started fiddling with the panel there, I got suspicious." He pointed to the external control panel for the engine room, to be used in case of accidents.

"With all that's been going on, how'd I know but maybe he was gonna dump the fuel? And then I seen he had keys. I didn't wait, sir. I jumped him. And then you come up."

Wilcox came from the background and dropped beside the still figure of Lomax. He opened the man's left hand and pulled out a bunch of keys, examining them. "Engine keys, Captain Muller. Hey—it's my set! He must have lifted them from my pocket. It looks as if Grundy's found our killer!"

"Or Lomax found him!" I pointed out. "Anybody else see this start, or know that Lomax didn't get those keys away from Grundy, when *he* started trouble?"

"Why, you—" Grundy began, but Wilcox cut off his run. It was a shame. I still felt like pushing the man's Adam's apple through his medulla oblongata.

"Lock them both up, until Dr. Lomax comes to," Muller ordered. "And send Dr. Napier to take care of him. I'm not jumping to any conclusions." But the look he was giving Lomax indicated that he'd already pretty well made up his mind. And the crew was positive. They drew back sullenly, staring at us like animals studying a human hunter, and they didn't like it when Peters took Grundy to lock him into his room. Muller finally chased them out, and left Wilcox and me alone.

Wilcox shrugged wryly, brushing dirt off his too-clean uniform. "While you're here, Tremaine, why not look my section over? You've been neglecting me."

I'd borrowed Muller's keys and inspected the engine room from, top to bottom the night before, but I didn't mention that. I hesitated now; to a man who grew up to be an engineer and who'd now gotten over his psychosis against space too late to start over, the engines were things better left alone. Then I remembered that I hadn't seen Wilcox's quarters, since he had the only key to them.

I nodded and went inside. The engines were old, and the gravity generator was one of the first models. But Wilcox knew his business. The place was slick enough, and there was the good clean smell of metal working right. I could feel the controls in my hands, and my nerves itched as I went about making a perfunctory token examination. I even opened the fuel lockers and glanced in. The two crewmen watched with hard eyes, slitted as tight as Grundy's, but they didn't bother me. Then I shrugged, and went back with Wilcox to his tiny cabin.

I was hit by the place before I got inside. Tiny, yes, but fixed up like the dream of every engineer. Clean, neat, filled with books and luxuries. He even had a tape player I'd seen on sale for a trifle over three thousand dollars. He turned it on, letting the opening bars of Haydn's Oxford Symphony come out. It was a binaural, ultra-fidelity job, and I could close my eyes and feel the orchestra in front of me.

This time I was thorough, right down the line, from the cabinets that held luxury food and wine to the little drawer where he kept his dress-suit studs; they might have been rutiles, but I had a hunch they were genuine catseyes.

He laughed when I finished, and handed me a glass of the first decent wine I'd tasted in months. "Even a small ozonator to make the air seem more breathable, and a dehumidifier, Tremaine. I like to live decently. I started saving my money once with the idea of getting a ship of my own—" There was a real dream in his eyes for a second. Then he shrugged. "But ships got bigger and more expensive. So I decided to live. At forty, I've got maybe twenty years ahead here, and I mean to enjoy it. And—well, there are ways of making a bit extra...."

I nodded. So it's officially smuggling to carry a four-ounce Martian fur to Earth where it's worth a fortune, considering the legal duty. But most officers did it now and then. He put on Sibelius' Fourth while I finished the wine. "If this mess is ever over, Paul, or you get a chance, drop down," he said. "I like a man who knows good things—and I liked your reaction when you spotted that Haydn for Hohmann's recording. Muller pretends to know music, but he likes the flashiness of Möhlwehr."

Hell, I'd cut my eye teeth on that stuff; my father had been first violinist in an orchestra, and had considered me a traitor when I was born without perfect pitch. We talked about Sibelius for awhile, before I left to go out into the stinking rest of the ship. Grundy was sitting before the engines, staring at them. Wilcox had said the big ape liked to watch them move ... but he was supposed to be locked up.

---

I stopped by Lomax's door; the shutter was open, and I could see the big man writhing about, but he was apparently unconscious. Napier came back from somewhere, and nodded quickly.

"Concussion," he said. "He's still out, but it shouldn't be too serious."

"Grundy's loose." I'd expected surprise, but there was none. "Why?"

He shrugged. "Muller claimed he needed his mate free to handle the crew, and that there was no place the man could go. I think it was because the men are afraid they'll be outnumbered by your group." His mouth smiled, but it was suddenly bitter. "Jenny talked Pietro into agreeing with Muller."

Mess was on when I reached the group. I wasn't hungry. The wine had cut the edge from my appetite, and the slow increase of poison in the air was getting me, as it was the others. Sure, carbon dioxide isn't a real poison— but no organism can live in its own waste, all the same. I had a rotten headache. I sat there playing a little game I'd invented—trying to figure which ones I'd eliminate if some had to die. Jenny laughed up at Muller, and I added him to the list. Then I changed it, and put her in his place. I was getting sick of the little witch, though I knew it would be different if she'd been laughing up at me. And then, because of the sick-calf look on Bill Sanderson's face as he stared at Eve, I added him, though I'd always liked the guy. Eve, surprisingly, had as many guys after her as Jenny; but she didn't seem interested. Or maybe she did—she'd pulled her hair back and put on a dress that made her figure look good. Either flattery was working, or she was entering into the last-days feeling most of us had.

Napier came in and touched my shoulder. "Lomax is conscious, and he's asking for you," he said, too low for the others to hear.

I found the chemist conscious, all right, but sick—and scared. His face winced, under all the bandages, as I opened the door. Then he saw who it was, and relaxed. "Paul—what happened to me? The last I remember is going up to see that second batch of plants poisoned. But—well, this is something I must have got later...."

I told him, as best I could. "But don't you remember anything?"

"Not a thing about that. It's the same as Napier told me, and I've been trying to remember. Paul, you don't think—?"

I put a hand on his shoulder and pushed him back gently. "Don't be a damned fool, Hal. I know you're no killer."

"But somebody is, Paul. Somebody tried to kill me while I was unconscious!"

He must have seen my reaction. "They did, Paul. I don't know how I know—maybe I almost came to—but somebody tried to poke a stick through the door with a knife on it. They want to kill me."

I tried to calm him down until Napier came and gave him a sedative. The doctor seemed as sick about Hal's inability to remember as I was, though he indicated it was normal enough in concussion cases. "So is the hallucination," he added. "He'll be all right tomorrow."

In that, Napier was wrong. When the doctor looked in on him the next time, the big chemist lay behind a door that had been pried open, with a long galley knife through his heart. On the bloody sheet, his finger had traced something in his own blood.

"*It was....*" But the last "s" was blurred, and there was nothing more.

# IV

I don't know how many were shocked at Hal's death, or how many looked around and counted one less pair of lungs. He'd never been one of the men I'd envied the air he used, though, and I think most felt the same. For awhile, we didn't even notice that the air was even thicker.

Phil Riggs broke the silence following our inspection of Lomax's cabin. "That damned Bullard! I'll get him, I'll get him as sure as he got Hal!"

There was a rustle among the others, and a suddenly crystallized hate on their faces. But Muller's hoarse shout cut through the babble that began, and rose over even the anguished shrieking of the cook. "Shut up, the lot of you! Bullard couldn't have committed the other crimes. Any one of you is a better suspect. Stop snivelling, Bullard, this isn't a lynching mob, and it isn't going to be one!"

"What about Grundy?" Walt Harris yelled.

Wilcox pushed forward. "Grundy couldn't have done it. He's the logical suspect, but he was playing rummy with my men."

The two engine men nodded agreement, and we began filing back to the mess hall, with the exception of Bullard, who shoved back into a niche, trying to avoid us. Then, when we were almost out of his sight, he let out a shriek and came blubbering after us.

I watched them put Hal Lomax's body through the 'tween-hulls lock, and turned toward the engine room; I could use some of that wine, just as the ship could have used a trained detective. But the idea of watching helplessly while the engines purred along to remind me I was just a handyman for the rest of my life got mixed up with the difficulty of breathing the stale air, and I started to turn back. My head was throbbing, and for two cents I'd have gone out between the hulls beside Lomax and the others and let the foul air spread out there and freeze....

The idea was slow coming. Then I was running back toward the engines. I caught up with Wilcox just before he went into his own quarters. "Wilcox!"

He swung around casually, saw it was me, and motioned inside. "How about some Bartok, Paul? Or would you rather soothe your nerves with some first-rate Buxtehude organ...."

"Damn the music," I told him. "I've got a wild idea to get rid of this carbon dioxide, and I want to know if we can get it working with what we've got."

He snapped to attention at that. Half-way through my account, he fished around and found a bottle of Armagnac. "I get it. If we pipe our air through the passages between the hulls on the shadow side, it will lose its heat in a hurry. And we can regulate its final temperature by how fast we pipe it through—just keep it moving enough to reach the level where carbon dioxide freezes out, but the oxygen stays a gas. Then pass it around the engines—we'll have to cut out the normal cooling set-up, but that's okay—warm it up.... Sure, I've got equipment enough for that. We can set it up in a day. Of course, it won't give us any more oxygen, but we'll be able to breathe what we have. To success, Paul!"

I guess it was good brandy, but I swallowed mine while calling Muller down, and never got to taste it.

It's surprising how much easier the air got to breathe after we'd double-checked the idea. In about fifteen minutes, we were all milling around in the engine room, while Wilcox checked through equipment. But there was no question about it. It was even easier than we'd thought. We could simply bypass the cooling unit, letting the engine housings stay open to the between-hulls section; then it was simply a matter of cutting a small opening into that section at the other end of the ship and installing a sliding section to regulate the amount of air flowing in. The exhaust from the engine heat pumps was reversed, and run out through a hole hastily knocked in the side of the wall.

Naturally, we let it flow too fast at first. Space is a vacuum, which means it's a good insulator. We had to cut the air down to a trickle. Then Wilcox ran into trouble because his engines wouldn't cool with that amount of air. He went back to supervise a patched-up job of splitting the coolers into sections, which took time. But after that, we had it.

I went through the hatch with Muller and Pietro. With air there was no need to wear space suits, but it was so cold that we could take it for only a minute or so. That was long enough to see a faint, fine mist of dry ice snow falling. It was also long enough to catch a sight of the three bodies there. I didn't enjoy that, and Pietro gasped. Muller grimaced. When we came back, he sent Grundy in to move the bodies to a hull-section where our breathing air wouldn't pass over them. It wasn't necessary, of course. But somehow, it seemed important.

By lunch, the air seemed normal. We shipped only pure oxygen at about three pounds pressure, instead of loading it with a lot of useless nitrogen. With the carbon dioxide cut back to normal levels, it was as good as ever. The only difference was that the fans had to be set to blow in a different pattern. We celebrated, and even Bullard seemed to have perked up. He dug out pork chops and almost succeeded in making us cornbread out of some coarse flour I saw him pouring out of the food chopper. He had perked up enough to bewail the fact that all he had was canned spinach instead of turnip greens.

But by night, the temper had changed—and the food indicated it again. Bullard's cooking was turning into a barometer of the psychic pressure. We'd had time to realize that we weren't getting something for nothing. Every molecule of carbon-dioxide that crystallized out took two atoms of oxygen with it, completely out of circulation.

---

We were also losing water-vapor, we found; normally, any one of our group knew enough science to know that the water would fall out before the carbon dioxide, but we hadn't thought of it. We took care of that, however, by having Wilcox weld in a baffle and keep the section where the water condensed separate from the carbon dioxide snowfall. We could always shovel out the real ice, and meantime the ship's controls restored the moisture to the air easily enough.

But there was nothing we could do about the oxygen. When that was gone, it stayed gone. The plants still took care of about two-thirds of our waste— but the other third was locked out there between the hulls. Given plants enough, we could have thawed it and let them reconvert it; a nice idea, except that we had to wait three months to take care of it, if we lived that long.

Bullard's cooking began to get worse. Then suddenly, we got one good meal. Eve Nolan came down the passage to announce that Bullard was making cake, with frosting, canned huckleberry pie, and all the works. We headed for the mess hall, fast.

It was the cook's masterpiece. Muller came down late, though, and regarded it doubtfully. "There's something funny," he said as he settled down beside me. Jenny had been surrounded by Napier and Pietro. "Bullard came up babbling a few minutes ago. I don't like it. Something about eating hearty, because he'd saved us all, forever and ever. He told me the angels were on our side, because a beautiful angel with two halos came to him in his sleep and told him how to save us. I chased him back to the galley, but I don't like it."

Most of them had already eaten at least half of the food, but I saw Muller wasn't touching his. The rest stopped now, as the words sank in, and Napier looked shocked. "No!" he said, but his tone wasn't positive. "He's a weakling, but I don't think he's insane—not enough to poison us."

"There was that food poisoning before," Pietro said suddenly. "Paul, come along. And don't eat anything until we come back."

We broke the record getting to the galley. There Bullard sat, beaming happily, eating from a huge plate piled with the food he had cooked. I checked on it quickly—and there wasn't anything he'd left out. He looked up, and his grin widened foolishly.

"Hi, docs," he said. "Yes, sir, I knowed you'd be coming. It all came to me in a dream. Looked just like my wife twenty years ago, she did, with green and yellow halos. And she told it to me. Told me I'd been a good man, and nothing was going to happen to me. Not to good old Emery Bullard. Had it all figgered out."

He speared a big forkful of food and crammed it into his mouth, munching noisily. "Had it all figgered. Pop-corn. Best damned pop-corn you ever saw, kind they raise not fifty miles from where I was born. You know, I didn't useta like you guys. But now I love everybody. When we get to Saturn, I'm gonna make up for all the times I didn't give you pop-corn. We'll pop and we'll pop. And beans, too. I useta hate beans. Always beans on a ship. But now we're saved, and I love beans!"

He stared after us, half coming out of his seat. "Hey, docs, ain't you gonna let me tell you about it?"

"Later, Bullard," Pietro called back. "Something just came up. We want to hear all about it."

Inside the mess hall, he shrugged. "He's eating the food himself. If he's crazy, he's in a happy stage of it. I'm sure he isn't trying to poison us." He sat down and began eating, without any hesitation.

I didn't feel as sure, and suspected he didn't. But it was too late to back out. Together, we summarized what he'd told us, while Napier puzzled over it. Finally the doctor shrugged. "Visions. Euphoria. Disconnection with reality. Apparently something of a delusion that he's to save the world. I'm not a psychiatrist, but it sounds like insanity to me. Probably not dangerous. At least, while he wants to save us, we won't have to worry about the food. Still...."

Wilcox mulled it over, and resumed the eating he had neglected before.

"Grundy claimed he'd been down near the engine room, trying to get permission to pop something in the big pile. I thought Grundy was just getting his stories mixed up. But—pop-corn!"

"I'll have him locked in his cabin," Muller decided. He picked up the nearest handset, saw that it was to the galley, and switched quickly. "Grundy, lock Bullard up. And no rough stuff this time." Then he turned to Napier. "Dr. Napier, you'll have to see him and find out what you can."

I guess there's a primitive fear of insanity in most of us. We felt sick, beyond the nagging worry about the food. Napier got up at once. "I'll give him a sedative. Maybe it's just nerves, and he'll snap out of it after a good sleep. Anyhow, your mate can stand watching."

"Who can cook?" Muller asked. His eyes swung down the table toward Jenny.

I wondered how she'd get out of that. Apparently she'd never told Muller about the scars she still had from spilled grease, and how she'd never forgiven her mother or been able to go near a kitchen since. But I should have guessed. She could remember my stories, too. Her eyes swung up toward mine pleadingly.

Eve Nolan stood up suddenly. "I'm not only a good cook, but I enjoy it," she stated flatly, and there was disgust in the look she threw at Jenny. She swung toward me. "How about it, Paul, can you wrestle the big pots around for me?"

"I used to be a short order cook when I was finishing school," I told her. But she'd ruined the line. The grateful look and laugh from Jenny weren't needed now. And curiously, I felt grateful to Eve for it. I got up and went after Napier.

I found him in Bullard's little cubbyhole of a cabin. He must have chased Grundy off, and now he was just drawing a hypo out of the cook's arm. "It'll take the pain away," he was saying softly. "And I'll see that he doesn't hit you again. You'll be all right, now. And in the morning, I'll come and listen to you. Just go to sleep. Maybe she'll come back and tell you more."

He must have heard me, since he signalled me out with his hand, and backed out quietly himself, still talking. He shut the door, and clicked the lock.

Bullard heard it, though. He jerked to a sitting position, and screamed. "*No! No! He'll kill me! I'm a good man....*"

He hunched up on the bed, forcing the sheet into his mouth. When he looked up a second later, his face was frozen in fear, but it was a desperate, calm kind of fear. He turned to face us, and his voice raised to a full shout, with every word as clear as he could make it.

"All right. Now I'll never tell you the secret. Now you can all die without air. I promise I'll never tell you what I know!"

He fell back, beating at the sheet with his hand and sobbing hysterically. Napier watched him. "Poor devil," the doctor said at last. "Well, in another minute the shot will take effect. Maybe he's lucky. He won't be worrying for awhile. And maybe he'll be rational tomorrow."

"All the same, I'm going to stand guard until Muller gets someone else here," I decided. I kept remembering Lomax.

Napier nodded, and half an hour later Bill Sanderson came to take over the watch. Bullard was sleeping soundly.

The next day, though, he woke up to start moaning and writing again. But he was keeping his word. He refused to answer any questions. Napier looked worried as he reported he'd given the cook another shot of sedative. There was nothing else he could do.

Cooking was a relief, in a way. By the time Eve and I had scrubbed all the pots into what she considered proper order, located some of the food lockers, and prepared and served a couple of meals, we'd evolved a smooth system that settled into a routine with just enough work to help keep our minds off the dwindling air in the tanks. In anything like a kitchen, she lost most of her mannish pose and turned into a live, efficient woman. And she could cook.

"First thing I learned," she told me. "I grew up in a kitchen. I guess I'd never have turned to photography if my kid brother hadn't been using our sink for his darkroom."

Wilcox brought her a bottle of his wine to celebrate her first dinner. He seemed to want to stick around, but she chased him off after the first drink. We saved half the bottle to make a sauce the next day.

It never got made. Muller called a council of war, and his face was pinched and old. He was leaning on Jenny as Eve and I came into the mess hall; oddly, she seemed to be trying to buck him up. He got down to the facts as soon as all of us were together.

"Our oxygen tanks are empty," he announced. "They shouldn't be—but they are. Someone must have sabotaged them before the plants were poisoned—and done it so the dials don't show it. I just found it out when the automatic switch to a new tank failed to work. We now have the air in the ship, and no more. Dr. Napier and I have figured that this will keep us all alive with the help of the plants for no more than fifteen days. I am open to any suggestions!"

There was silence after that, while it soaked in. Then it was broken by a thin scream from Phil Riggs. He slumped into a seat and buried his head in his hands. Pietro put a hand on the man's thin shoulders, "Captain Muller—"

"Kill 'em!" It was Grundy's voice, bellowing sharply. "Let'em breathe space! They got us into it! We can make out with the plants left! It's our ship!"

Muller had walked forward. Now his fist lashed out, and Grundy crumpled. He lay still for a second, then got to his feet unsteadily. Jenny screamed, but Muller moved steadily back to his former place without looking at the mate. Grundy hesitated, fumbled in his pocket for something, and swallowed it.

"Captain, sir!" His voice was lower this time.

"Yes, Mr. Grundy?"

"How many of us can live off the plants?"

"Ten—perhaps eleven."

"Then—then give us a lottery!"

Pietro managed to break in over the yells of the rest of the crew. "I was about to suggest calling for volunteers, Captain Muller. I still have enough faith in humanity to believe...."

"You're a fool, Dr. Pietro," Muller said flatly. "Do you think Grundy would volunteer? Or Bullard? But thanks for clearing the air, and admitting your group has nothing more to offer. A lottery seems to be the only fair system."

He sat down heavily. "We have tradition on this; in an emergency such as this, death lotteries have been held, and have been considered legal afterwards. Are there any protests?"

I could feel my tongue thicken in my mouth. I could see the others stare about, hoping someone would object, wondering if this could be happening. But nobody answered, and Muller nodded reluctantly. "A working force must be left. Some men are indispensable. We must have an engineer, a navigator, and a doctor. One man skilled with engine-room practice and one with deck work must remain."

"And the cook goes," Grundy yelled. His eyes were intent and slitted again.

Some of both groups nodded, but Muller brought his fist down on the table. "This will be a legal lottery, Mr. Grundy. Dr. Napier will draw for him."

"And for myself," Napier said. "It's obvious that ten men aren't going on to Saturn—you'll have to turn back, or head for Jupiter. Jupiter, in fact, is the only sensible answer. And a ship can get along without a doctor that long when it has to. I demand my right to the draw."

Muller only shrugged and laid down the rules. They were simple enough. He would cut drinking straws to various lengths, and each would draw one. The two deck hands would compare theirs, and the longer would be automatically safe. The same for the pair from the engine-room. Wilcox was safe. "Mr. Peters and I will also have one of us eliminated," he added quietly. "In an emergency, our abilities are sufficiently alike."

The remaining group would have their straws measured, and the seven shortest ones would be chosen to remove themselves into a vacant section between hulls without air within three hours, or be forcibly placed there. The remaining ten would head for Jupiter if no miracle removed the danger in those three hours.

Peters got the straws, and Muller cut them and shuffled them. There was a sick silence that let us hear the sounds of the scissors with each snip. Muller arranged them so the visible ends were even. "Ladies first," he said. There was no expression on his face or in his voice.

Jenny didn't giggle, but neither did she balk. She picked a straw, and then shrieked faintly. It was obviously a long one. Eve reached for hers—

And Wilcox yelled suddenly. "Captain Muller, protest! Protest! You're using all long straws for the women!" He had jumped forward, and now struck down Muller's hand, proving his point.

"You're quite right, Mr. Wilcox," Muller said woodenly. He dropped his hand toward his lap and came up with a group of the straws that had been cut, placed there somehow without our seeing it. He'd done a smooth job of it, but not smooth enough. "I felt some of you would notice it, but I also felt that gentlemen would prefer to see ladies given the usual courtesies."

He reshuffled the assorted straws, and then paused. "Mr. Tremaine, there was a luxury liner named the *Lauri Ellu* with an assistant engineer by your name; and I believe you've shown a surprising familiarity with certain customs of space. A few days ago, Jenny mentioned something that jogged my memory. Can you still perform the duties of an engineer?"

Wilcox had started to protest at the delay. Now shock ran through him. He stared unbelievingly from Muller to me and back, while his face blanched. I could guess what it must have felt like to see certain safety cut to a 50 per cent chance, and I didn't like the way Muller was willing to forget until he wanted to take a crack at Wilcox for punishment. But....

"I can," I answered. And then, because I was sick inside myself for cutting under Wilcox, I managed to add, "But I—I waive my chance at immunity!"

"Not accepted," Muller decided. "Jenny, will you draw?"

It was pretty horrible. It was worse when the pairs compared straws. The animal feelings were out in the open then. Finally, Muller, Wilcox, and two crewmen dropped out. The rest of us went up to measure our straws.

It took no more than a minute. I stood staring down at the ruler, trying to stretch the tiny thing I'd drawn. I could smell the sweat rising from my body. But I knew the answer. I had three hours left!

---

"Riggs, Oliver, Nolan, Harris, Tremaine, Napier and Grundy," Muller announced.

A yell came from Grundy. He stood up, with the engine man named Oliver, and there was a gun in his hand. "No damned big brain's kicking me off my ship," he yelled. "You guys know me. Hey, *rooob!*"

Oliver was with him, and the other three of the crew sprang into the group. I saw Muller duck a shot from Grundy's gun, and leap out of the room. Then I was in it, heading for Grundy. Beside me, Peters was trying to get a chair broken into pieces. I felt something hit my shoulder, and the shock knocked me downward, just as a shot whistled over my head.

Gravity cut off!

Someone bounced off me. I got a piece of the chair that floated by, found the end cracked and sharp, and tried to spin towards Grundy, but I couldn't see him. I heard Eve's voice yell over the other shouts. I spotted the plate coming for me, but I was still in midair. It came on steadily, edge on, and I felt it break against my forehead. Then I blacked out.

# V

I had the grandaddy of all headaches when I came to. Doc Napier's face was over me, and Jenny and Muller were working on Bill Sanderson. There was a surprisingly small and painful lump on my head. Pietro and Napier helped me up, and I found I could stand after a minute.

There were four bodies covered with sheets on the floor. "Grundy, Phil Riggs, Peters and a deckhand named Storm," Napier said. "Muller gave us a whiff of gas and not quite in time."

"Is the time up?" I asked. It was the only thing I could think of.

Pietro shook his head sickly. "Lottery is off. Muller says we'll have to hold another, since Storm and Peters were supposed to be safe. But not until tomorrow."

Eve came in then, lugging coffee. Her eyes found me, and she managed a brief smile. "I gave the others coffee," she reported to Muller. "They're pretty subdued now."

"Mutiny!" Muller helped Jenny's brother to his feet and began helping him toward the door. "Mutiny! And I have to swallow that!"

Pietro watched him go, and handed Eve back his cup. "And there's no way of knowing who was on which side. Dr. Napier, could you do something...."

He held out his hands that were shaking, and Napier nodded. "I can use a sedative myself. Come on back with me."

Eve and I wandered back to the kitchen. I was just getting my senses back. The damned stupidity of it all. And now it would have to be done over. Three of us still had to have our lives snuffed out so the others could live—and we all had to go through hell again to find out which.

Eve must have been thinking the same. She sank down on a little stool, and her hand came out to find mine. "For what? Paul, whoever poisoned the plants knew it would go this far! He had to! What's to be gained? Particularly when he'd have to go through all this, too! He must have been crazy!"

"Bullard couldn't have done it," I said slowly.

"Why should it be Bullard? How do we know he was insane? Maybe when he was shouting that he wouldn't tell, he was trying to make a bribe to save his own life. Maybe he's as scared as we are. Maybe he was making sense all along, if we'd only listened to him. He—"

She stood up and started back toward the lockers, but I caught her hand. "Eve, he wouldn't have done it—the killer—if he'd had to go through the lottery! He knew he was safe! That's the one thing we've been overlooking. The man to suspect is the only man who could be sure he would get back! My God, we saw him juggle those straws to save Jenny! He knew he'd control the lottery."

She frowned. "But ... Paul, he practically suggested the lottery! Grundy brought it up, but he was all ready for it." The frown vanished, then returned. "But I still can't believe it."

"He's the one who wanted to go back all the time. He kept insisting on it, but he had to get back without violating his contract." I grabbed her hand and started toward the nose of the ship, justifying it to her as I went. "The only man with a known motive for returning, the only one completely safe—and we didn't even think of it!"

She was still frowning, but I wasn't wasting time. We came up the corridor to the control room. Ahead the door was slightly open, and I could hear a mutter of Jenny's voice. Then there was the tired rumble of Muller.

"I'll find a way, baby. I don't care how close they watch, we'll make it work. Pick the straw with the crimp in the end—I can do that, even if I can't push one out further again. I tell you, nothing's going to happen to you."

"But Bill—" she began.

I hit the door, slamming it open. Muller sat on a narrow couch with Jenny on his lap. I took off for him, not wasting a good chance when he was handicapped. But I hadn't counted on Jenny. She was up, and her head banged into my stomach before I knew she was coming. I felt the wind knocked out, but I got her out of my way—to look up into the muzzle of a gun in Muller's hands.

"You'll explain this, Mr. Tremaine," he said coldly. "In ten seconds, I'll have an explanation or a corpse."

"Go ahead," I told him. "Shoot, damn you! You'll get away with this, too, I suppose. Mutiny, or something. And down in that rotten soul of yours, I suppose you'll be gloating at how you made fools of us. The only man on board who was safe even from a lottery, and we couldn't see it. Jenny, I hope you'll be happy with this butcher. Very happy!"

He never blinked. "Say that about the only safe man aboard again," he suggested.

I repeated it, with details. But he didn't like my account. He turned to Eve, and motioned for her to take it up. She was frowning harder, and her voice was uncertain, but she summed up our reasons quickly enough.

And suddenly Muller was on his feet. "Mr. Tremaine, for a damned idiot, you have a good brain. You found the key to the problem, even if you couldn't find the lock. Do you know what happens to a captain who permits a death lottery, even what I called a legal one? He doesn't captain a liner—he shoots himself after he delivers his ship, if he's wise! Come on, we'll find the one indispensable man. You stay here, Jenny—you too, Eve!"

Jenny whimpered, but stayed. Eve followed, and he made no comment. And then it hit me. The man who had *thought* he was indispensable, and hence safe—the man I'd naturally known in the back of my head could be replaced, though no one else had known it until a little while ago.

"He must have been sick when you ran me in as a ringer," I said, as we walked down toward the engine hatch. "But why?"

"I've just had a wild guess as to part of it," Muller said.

---

Wilcox was listening to the Buxtehude when we shoved the door of his room open, and he had his head back and eyes closed. He snapped to attention, and reached out with one hand toward a drawer beside him. Then he dropped his arm and stood up, to cut off the tape player.

"Mr. Wilcox," Muller said quietly, holding the gun firmly on the engineer. "Mr. Wilcox, I've detected evidence of some of the Venus drugs on your two assistants for some time. It's rather hard to miss the signs in their eyes. I've also known that Mr. Grundy was an addict. I assumed that they were getting it from him naturally. And as long as they performed their duties, I couldn't be choosy on an old ship like this. But for an officer to furnish such drugs—and to smuggle them from Venus for sale to other planets—is something I cannot tolerate. It will make things much simpler if you will surrender those drugs to me. I presume you keep them in those bottles of wine you bring aboard?"

Wilcox shook his head slowly, settling back against the tape machine. Then he shrugged and bowed faintly. "The chianti, sir!"

I turned my head toward the bottles, and Eve started forward. Then I yelled as Wilcox shoved his hand down toward the tape machine. The gun came out on a spring as he touched it.

Muller shot once, and the gun missed Wilcox's fingers as the engineer's hand went to his hip, where blood was flowing. He collapsed into the chair behind him, staring at the spot stupidly. "I cut my teeth on *tough* ships, Mr. Wilcox," Muller said savagely.

The man's face was white, but he nodded slowly, and a weak grin came onto his lips. "Maybe you didn't exaggerate those stories at that," he conceded slowly. "I take it I drew a short straw."

"Very short. It wasn't worth it. No profit from the piddling sale of drugs is worth it."

"There's a group of strings inside the number one fuel locker," Wilcox said between his teeth. The numbness was wearing off, and the shattered bones in his hip were beginning to eat at him. "Paul, pull up one of the packages and bring it here, will you?"

I found it without much trouble—along with a whole row of others, fine cords cemented to the side of the locker. The package I drew up weighed about ten pounds. Wilcox opened it and scooped out a thimbleful of greenish powder. He washed it down with wine.

"Fatal?" Muller asked.

The man nodded. "In that dosage, after a couple of hours. But it cuts out the pain—ah, better already. I won't feel it. Captain, I was never piddling. Your ship has been the sole source of this drug to Mars since a year or so after I first shipped on her. There are about seven hundred pounds of pure stuff out there. Grundy and the others would commit public murder daily rather than lose the few ounces a year I gave them. Imagine what would happen when Pietro conscripted the *Wahoo* and no drugs arrived. The addicts find out no more is coming—they look for the peddlers—and *they* start looking for their suppliers...."

He shrugged. "There might have been time and ways, if I could have gotten the ship back to Earth or Jupiter. It might have been recommissioned into the Earth-Mars-Venus run, even. Pietro's injunction caught me before I could transship, but with another chance, I might have gotten the stuff to Mars in time.... Well, it was a chance I took. Satisfied?"

---

Eve stared at him with horrified eyes. Maybe I was looking the same. It was plain enough now. He'd planned to poison the plants and drive us back. Murder of Hendrix had been a blunder when he'd thought it wasn't working properly. "What about Sam?" I asked.

"Blackmail. He was too smart. He'd been sure Grundy was smuggling the stuff, and raking off from him. He didn't care who killed Hendrix as much as how much Grundy would pay to keep his mouth shut—with murder around, he figured Grundy'd get rattled. The fool did, and Sam smelled bigger stakes. Grundy was bait to get him down near here. I killed him."

"And Lomax?"

"I don't know. Maybe he was bluffing. But he kept going from room to room with a pocketful of chemicals, making some kind of tests. I couldn't take a chance on his being able to spot chromazone. So I had Grundy give him my keys and tell him to go ahead—then jump him."

And after that, when he wasn't quite killed, they'd been forced to finish the job. Wilcox shrugged again. "I guess it got out of hand. I'll make a tape of the whole story for you, Captain. But I'd appreciate it if you'd get Napier down here. This is getting pretty messy."

"He's on the way," Eve said. We hadn't seen her call, but the doctor arrived almost immediately afterwards.

He sniffed the drug, and questioned us about the dose Wilcox had taken. Then he nodded slowly. "About two hours, I'd say. No chance at all to save him. The stuff is absorbed almost at once and begins changing to something else in the blood. I'll be responsible, if you want."

Muller shrugged. "I suppose so. I'd rather deliver him in irons to a jury, but.... Well, we still have a lottery to hold!"

It jerked us back to reality sharply. Somehow, I'd been fighting off the facts, figuring that finding the cause would end the results. But even with Wilcox out of the picture, there were twelve of us left—and air for only ten!

Wilcox laughed abruptly. "A favor for a favor. I can give you a better answer than a lottery."

"Pop-corn! Bullard!" Eve slapped her head with her palm. "Captain, give me the master key." She snatched it out of his hand and was gone at a run.

Wilcox looked disappointed, and then grinned. "Pop-corn and beans. I overlooked them myself. We're a bunch of city hicks. But when Bullard forgot his fears in his sleep, he remembered the answer—and got it so messed up with his dream and his new place as a hero that my complaint tipped the balance. Grundy put the fear of his God into him then. And you didn't get it. Captain, you don't dehydrate beans and pop-corn—they come that way naturally. You don't can them, either, if you're saving weight. They're seeds—put them in tanks and they grow!"

He leaned back, trying to laugh at us, as Napier finished dressing his wound. "Bullard knows where the lockers are. And corn grows pretty fast. It'll carry you through. Do I get that favor? It's simple enough—just to have Beethoven's Ninth on the machine and for the whole damned lot of you to get out of my cabin and let me die in my own way!"

Muller shrugged, but Napier found the tape and put it on. I wanted to see the louse punished for every second of worry, for Lomax, for Hendrix— even for Grundy. But there wasn't much use in vengeance at this point.

"You're to get all this, Paul," Wilcox said as we got ready to leave. "Captain Muller, everything here goes to Tremaine. I'll make a tape on that, too. But I want it to go to a man who can appreciate Hohmann's conducting."

Muller closed the door. "I guess it's yours," he admitted. "Now that you're head engineer here, Mr. Tremaine, the cabin is automatically yours. Take over. And get that junk in the fuel locker cleaned out—except enough to keep your helpers going. They'll need it, and we'll need their work."

"I'll clean out his stuff at the same time," I said. "I don't want any part of it."

He smiled then, just as Eve came down with Bullard and Pietro. The fat cook was sobered, but already beginning to fill with his own importance. I caught snatches as they began to discuss Bullard's knowledge of growing things. It was enough to know that we'd all live, though it might be tough for a while.

Then Muller gestured upwards. "You've got a reduced staff, Dr. Pietro. Do you intend going on to Saturn?"

"We'll go on," Pietro decided. And Muller nodded. They turned and headed upwards.

I stood staring at my engines. One of them was a touch out of phase and I went over and corrected it. They'd be mine for over two years—and after that, I'd be back on the lists.

Eve came over beside me, and studied them with me. Finally she sighed softly. "I guess I can see why you feel that way about them, Paul," she said. "And I'll be coming down to look at them. But right now, Bullard's too busy to cook, and everyone's going to be hungry when they find we're saved."

I chuckled, and felt the relief wash over me finally. I dropped my hand from the control and caught hers—a nice, friendly hand.

But at the entrance I stopped and looked back toward the cabin where Wilcox lay. I could just make out the second movement of the Ninth beginning.

I never could stand the cheap blatancy of Hohmann's conducting.

CPSIA information can be obtained
at www.ICGtesting.com
Printed in the USA
LVHW110933221222
735718LV00005B/375